The Walk

'It is only ideas gained from walking
that have any worth.'

Friedrich Nietzsche

king Soci

Contents

ety believ

Walking means travelling, physically moving from one place to another. In a metaphoric sense it also means advancing, exploring, developing, improving, innovating.

Society is less focused on the individual as it represents a community, the people, citizenship: it stands for humanity at large.

The Walking Society, it follows, refers to a circle of like-minded fellows, of ramblers and amblers, who take pleasure in exploring their surroundings on foot. As much as anything, the Walking Society is also an attitude: 'A spiritual society that is open to all people who, coming from diverse social, cultural, economic, or geographical realities, and who, individually or collectively, dedicate their imagination and energy to bringing useful and positive ideas and alternative solutions for a better world.'

With these words Camper manifests its understanding of today's life led on foot, and invites the reader to stroll through forty years of the company's history. The book begins in 1975, when Lorenzo Fluxa founded the company on the island of Mallorca, named it after the Mallorcan word for *peasant*, and launched its first shoe, inspired by the footwear worn in the island's rural countryside. Paired with a unique way of humorous and bold communication and the introduction of a radical store concept, Fluxa set the ground rules for the business of everyday shoes, shoes that defy category but serve the simple purpose of walking.

'Walking is freedom,' says philosopher Frédéric Gros. 'It is an escape, a temporary disconnection from our daily lives.' The freedom to go your own way, to stop and experiment, or to go on and try something new, to sidetrack. But perhaps most important of all it is the freedom to go at your own speed. It is a kind of 'good slowness, the sort of slowness that isn't exactly the opposite to speed,' writes Gros and continues: 'Walking is not a sport.' Sport is a discipline, an ethic, a labour. Walking, on the other hand, 'is the best way to go more slowly than any other method that has ever been found. If you want to go faster, then don't walk.'[1]

There is no rush, in walking or in good business. Therefore this book is foremost a celebration of a family business. Synonymous with independence that allows a brand to be flexible in its decisions, to experiment and to surprise with unexpected new endeavours, it is about an attitude towards business and the world. Camper does not set out to revolutionize, it searches for an alternative that is always personal.

In all this the remoteness of an island in the Mediterranean Sea could be interpreted as a hindrance. But it is quite the opposite. Mallorca and its austerity, with its contrast between idyllic nature and mass tourism, keeps heritage and traditional values alive, and allows for a clear position on fleeting trends in the fashion centers of the world. Mallorca in fact has enabled the little local company Camper to become successful on a global level.

Reading this book should be like taking a walk. Conceived as a promenade, readers can choose to begin wherever they like and continue in any direction, rambling through, taking shortcuts, skipping sections, or retracing their steps. They may rush through some sequences, then slow down and let the mind wander, before picking up the road again. This book is for wanderers and wonderers.

1 Frédéric Gros, *A Philosophy of Walking*. Verso Books: London, 2014, p. 1 (Kindle edition).

For a family business, the long term is one of the most important assets to be preserved.

I received from my father and grandfather a legacy of quality and values. In 1877 my grandfather Antonio founded a small workshop in Mallorca and years later mechanized the process to produce Goodyear welt quality shoes. My father expanded the production and converted the workshop into one of the best shoe factories in Spain for high-quality traditional men's shoes. I joined my father and my brother in 1970 to learn the secrets and know-how of the family business. In 1975 Spain recovered democracy after forty years, and in its wake came a storm of enthusiasm, freedom, and projects with a common will to modernize the country.

Within this atmosphere we launched Camper in 1975 with the support of a one-hundred-year-old tradition behind us and two main ideas in mind: first, to build an original casual brand from the Mediterranean adding to the comfort shoe a lot of imagination, irony, and innovation through a contemporary design; the second, to be an open house for creative people from diverse areas: footwear design, advertising, interior design and architecture, graphic design, photography, environmentalism, and materials. The idea to work together with a creative network, experts, and artisans has been something crucial from the beginning and this diversity gives the brand a certain contradiction within a coherence.

When, in 1992, we opened our first shop outside of Spain, in Paris, we were aware that this would be a difficult and long way, but we wanted to show the world our identity, built on a small island in the middle of the Mediterranean, away from the trends and influence of the international fashion circuit. Our motto, 'Walk don't run,' describes that spirit.

The Fluxa family's shoemaking legacy spans four generations. In 1877 Antonio Fluxa travelled to England to study modern shoe production. Upon his return he set up Mallorca's first industrial shoe manufacture (1903).

I would like to thank everyone who has contributed to building this company. Much of their work is reflected in this book. Looking back, I'm happy to see how Camper has grown from a local to an international company while remaining loyal to its origins and values and maintaining a cultural and human approach to business.

Values are possibly the greatest legacy to leave to the next generations. What we believe in will greatly impact what our future world will be like. There is still a lot to do, a lot to improve, but there is an exciting time ahead. I'm certain that the fourth generation of our family will lead, by their example and commitment, the family business to the next level – discreetly, with humour, and with imagination.

es walkin

After the change in the political situation in 1975, Spanish society began to change rapidly. A new spirit of freedom and peace spread over the country; the island of Mallorca became a favourite tourist destination. Shoes, however, stayed the same: classic and serious. The Camaleón was the first shoe to break with this hierarchical tradition. Modeled after the typical shoes worn in the countryside, it featured uppers crafted from canvas and leather offcuts and rubber soles made from tires. The perfect expression of the new spirit, Camper's modern shoe inspired by the rural past became a cult item among international visitors. Yet it was not easy to introduce this kind of shoe into the traditional footwear business, which was struggling with concepts like casual and unisex footwear.

Lorenzo Fluxa
Founder

'Casual footwear was unheard of in 1970s Spain, let alone unisex! We wanted to break with traditional typologies. That's what we have been doing ever since – never perfect, but always a little better.'

Groovy

Ranger

Camper

Harley

Walker

19   Spain in the 1970s felt like a country with something to prove. Everything that came or appeared to come from abroad was valued highly because it conveyed modernity. To decide on the name for the new company, Lorenzo Fluxa commissioned a survey: 'Groovy' won first place, closely followed by 'Ranger'. In the end the most authentic name on the list was chosen, even if it came in third: 'Camper', which simply means 'peasant' in Mallorcan.

20 Next a logo had to be created for the newly found brand. The first Western look, designed
by Alfonso Martín, included '1877' – the year the Fluxa family started their shoemaking business.
Over the years Camper's logo has evolved and the typeface has been updated.

21   Carlos Rolando introduced the bridge shape and colour (Pantone 485) in 1981, in order to apply
the logo also to shop signage. The new bold design allowed for better visibility, attracting passers-by.
The most recent, minimalistic red, white, or black variations have omitted the company's name
completely to a simple yet strong symbol.

Camper wanted to explain to society that their products are not just shoes, but rather a way of (walking through) life. Relaxed, humorous, bordering on irreverent, and deliberately complex. Carlos Rolando and publicist Joaquín Lorente, co-founder of the MMLB agency, created an advertising strategy for Camper, like this Camaleón advert from 1976: 'At first glance it's slapdash luxury, half Biscúter [a Spanish microcar known as the Zapatilla, or 'little shoe'], half Rolls-Royce.'

A Calendar from 1978.

'In the 1970s, shoe shopping was a complicated undertaking. Shoes were only displayed in the shop window. Inside, you had to find an assistant, point out the shoe you liked, then wait while she looked for your size in the storage room. We introduced "serve yourself" to shoe shopping.'

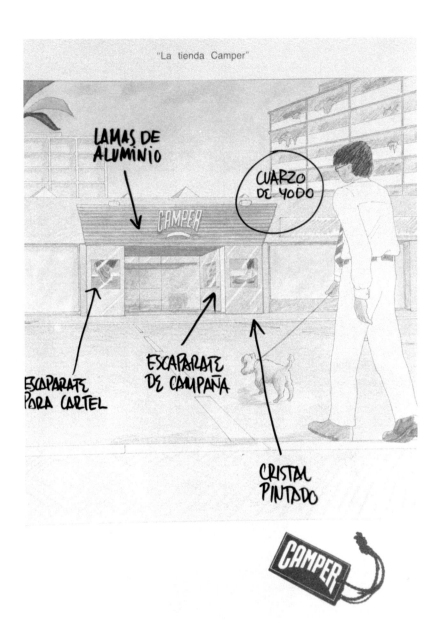

It was up to Fernando Amat, owner of Barcelona's famed Vinçon store, to devise an entirely new type of shoe store. Working with interior designer Olé Armengol, scenographer Jordi Nogués, and a sociologist, Amat thoroughly analysed the existing retail culture and customer behaviour to create a distinctive setting for its products and a more immersive shopping experience free of old-fashioned formalities.

In Fall 1981 the first Camper store opened in Barcelona's trendy Calle Muntaner. The store was easily recognizable thanks to its garage-like appearance and bright red sign. The entrance area was used for theatrical window displays.

Posters on the outside façade were changed on a regular basis. 'We used posters in the same way cinemas do, to let people know what film is playing,' explains graphic designer Rolando.

28   Inside, shoes were lined up on shelves within easy reach so that customers could look, choose, touch, and try them on. The original carpet, designed by Javier Mariscal, squeaked like frogs with every step. The shop's interior was an ever-changing stage and Amat's original concept could be applied to different spaces. Yet his ambitious idea to change the layout, including the flooring, on a frequent basis proved to be too complicated with the increasing number of new shops.

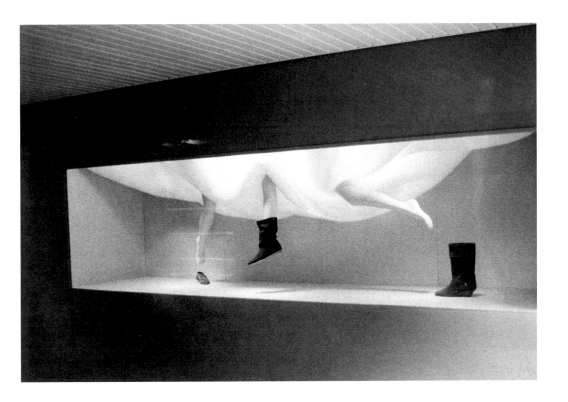

29   Every window display was a little piece of imaginative theatre in its own right, showing that buying shoes could also be fun and culturally enriching. But most important, window displays were a tool of communication. The sets were created and updated for every new collection by Jordi Nogués.

30   In addition to shops, ads, and posters, shopping bags and shoeboxes became important vehicles for conveying a message. These were simple and efficient, like the slogans printed on the first bags: 'I come from Camper', followed by 'Tomorrow I'll wear Camper for the first time.' This was the first time the logo's symbolic bridge appeared without the name; it would be many years before this version of the logo was used regularly.

31   Collected by some, overlooked by many, the cardboard shoebox is an important element of protection
and storage. Once it leaves the store It also becomes an important means of communication.
Graphically similar to the ads, the first shoebox looks like it was wrapped in newspaper.

USE ZAPATOS. ES MAS COMODO.

32   The arrival of Camper-only stores brought about a change in the brand's communication, as posters at
the stores became the key tool, as exemplified in this poster by Joaquin Lorente: 'Wear shoes. It's more
comfortable.' The foundation of the company was laid: A name that relates to origin and place, a functional
product, a humorous communication strategy, and an innovative retail concept.

g should l

be like lea

fing com

'Where do you want to go?' Sami asked her wordlessly. And Ora lifted her chin and said, also in silence: 'Go ahead, further.' They are walking. Sami and Ora are two characters from David Grossman's novel *To the End of the Land*, who walk for endless miles to flee from news that they may or may not receive. In fact, it is Ora who is fleeing – Sami is only keeping her company, like a shadow of her flight, or a shadow of the shadow of another, older flight. Ora has decided to become 'the first conscientious objector to news'. She has decided not to be at home on the day that a soldier arrives at her door to tell her that her son has been killed at the front. She goes to roam around, with no telephone number or address, as a way of refusing to accept the slightest possibility that this (the violent death and the violent news) will occur. Her stream of consciousness becomes a monologue with her own memory and a dialogue with Sami. Like all of us, they are walking to remember, to think and to talk – or rather, to change the subject. It has been scientifically proven that we are incapable of advancing in a straight line and that we have a tendency to walk in circles, in a never-ending succession of detours, crossroads, and diversions.

Ora is a 'no' pilgrim. Her stance is profoundly political. She is continuing a tradition embraced by thousands before her, including many a prestigious individual. Mildred Norman, the Pilgrim of Peace, was one: she covered some 40,000 kilometres of the United States on foot in a period of 28 years. Another was Henry David Thoreau, who was an advocate of submissiveness and walking in practice as well as in principle. As they did, Ora refuses to accept the maxims imposed by the ruling social order. Assertive by nature, she rejects them wholeheartedly. The normative road map has disappeared, with its clear outline of what others expect, because they are subject to State control. Later in the story, her actions display the faith of those who abandon their countries and believe in an overarching shared and often international space, built of energy and dust and accessed through the transcendence of movement. It cannot be a mere coincidence that all of the major religions share a belief in the importance of pilgrimage and a holy book. Faith in the otherworldly, however, has two real-world interpretations: in the feet and the eyes, in the path and the word, in walking and reading. On her pilgrimage, Ora seeks to marry faith with action and the abstract with the concrete: every step is like a prayer or an incantation that she hopes will prevent her son's death. Ora's trek echoes that of Werner Herzog, who walked over 800 kilometres from Munich to Paris to rail against a friend's illness and death.

Four hundred pages later, Sami decides to turn back: 'I'm going to read a book about Galilee, or maybe it will be enough if I look at a map. I want to know where I've been.' But it turns out to be impossible to say for certain, because maps deal with space, whereas walking, first and foremost, takes place in time.

Bruce Chatwin reminds us that walking involves moving at a natural human velocity set by the rhythm of our heartbeat and breathing. Like so many writers and thinkers before him, he wanted to believe that walking is the infallible cure for boredom and melancholy. Heir to Walter Benjamin and Osip Mandelstam, the British writer was both a great storyteller and an unsystematic travel theorist, who argued that human nature is more nomadic than it is sedentary.

The birth of the city, when Cain killed Abel, pushed us towards private property and crime, walls and state boundaries, the police and the army. But it also brought with it two incredible realities: the chance to walk in an urban setting and, above all, the invention of the park, countryside, and nature. All provide a perfect backdrop for walking.

Chatwin's biographer, Susannah Clapp, adapted his surname as a shorthand; *chatwinesque* is an adjective meaning 'fruit of the connection between two highly improbable coincidences'. That is what W. G. Sebald does during the epic trek that forms the backbone of his book *The Rings of Saturn*. In utterly chatwinesque style, the intelligent writer decides to connect everything that he views as highly suited to connections. From Borges to the burning of the Amazon rainforest; from the cloth trade in Norwich to the art of sericulture in ancient China and its resurgence under the Nazis; from hotels that take refuge in harking back to the decline of the bourgeoisie to Rembrandt's *The Anatomy Lesson*. For centuries we walked to connect with objects that seemed worlds away. It is no coincidence that modern poetry was born with a poem by Charles Baudelaire, 'Correspondences', in which the writer is someone who walks the earth, crossing forests of symbols in search of the familiar, of a link between elements that only he can intertwine with one another.

'Adventures' is the title of the first part of a book of essays called *Passing the Baton* by another great travel writer – also a film-maker whose perspective is always a travelling shot – Edgardo Cozarinsky. In another of his works, *Rothschild's Violin*, we find this illuminating passage: 'Fiction often emerges as a way of questioning the facts. I would add my own *never stop questioning* to Forster's *only*

'To be away from home and yet to feel oneself everywhere at home; to see the world, to be at the centre of the world, and yet to remain hidden from the world. The spectator is a prince who everywhere rejoices in his incognito.' Charles Baudelaire's description of the flâneur.

connect: when we try to uncover hidden links, continuity, and logic or lack thereof, a plot – a crucial component – forces its way into the narrative.' The dictionary continues to warn us against the concept of a 'plot'. It still connotes a network of different threads, or a fabric, at the heart of which there may be a trap to be caught up in. However, it also connotes the concept of a blossoming of ideas. It is as if the act of writing a plot covered up a secret: as if weaving a fabric or writing were actions that could only be completed by stealth. The same happens with the spatial writing known as walking. Although we can describe a route using coordinates, steps, or words, there is always an inherent and inaccessible mystery that

'My first work made by walking, in 1967, was a straight line in a grass field, which was also my own path, going "nowhere." My intention was to make a new art which was also a new way of walking: walking as art.' Richard Long

is shrouded in the physical experience and its flickering spiritual translation. It is an experience that often leaves us in a mess – because of fatigue, chance encounters, or ideas.

Just like the distinguished naturalists who crossed oceans in the 18th century, like C. Auguste Dupin or Sherlock Holmes in the 19th-century metropolis, like Walter Benjamin, Guy Debord, and other philosophers in the centres and on the fringes of the 20th century, anyone who walks in the countryside or the city does so with a critical spirit. Through walking, our body acts as a link between locations (the woods and the quarry, the wrong and right sides of the tracks) that were theoretically disconnected previously. Modernity is an age in human history when the population approaches learning from the past as an exercise in forging links, finding common ground, searching for passageways, and crossing borders. By way of a parenthesis, suburban life has come to dominate certain places in the past few decades, with its residential neighbourhoods, hours and hours spent in cars, on urban roads and highways and leisure time shackled to the shopping centre. But in the 21st century, this concept of urbanism is in a state of decline. Following the postmodernity that celebrated Las Vegas and resigned itself to the non-place, walking and cycling are experiencing a revival. So too are pedestrian areas, the neighbourhood park, the coastal path as a natural extension of the port: all a kind of scale by which to judge the emotional framework of the city.

The ECG of a city bursts with red-letter days. Some of these are regular outbursts: carnivals, solstices, marathons or anniversaries. Others are unexpected, such as sporting finals or political rallies. Societies come together to jump, dance, or run in celebration; and to walk in indignation. There is political power in such demonstrations of collective force. Paradoxically, in the digital era, who can say whether this power has grown rather than declined? Bodies continue to be necessary.

'As a sceptic detective', writes Cozarinsky in the aforementioned book, 'I understood that the clues only allow us to discover something other than what we set out to find.' This logic is as applicable to walking as it is to writing and their sole opposite, which is reading. Reading a natural or urban landscape is a lot like translating, in that it involves searching for echoes and correspondences, equivalence and surprises. The term *wandering* implies always finding something that you did not set out to search for. It does not matter whether we do it on the shelves of a bookshop – that urban space where we walk through a miniature version of the city that surrounds us – on the pages of a book, in the maze that encircles the souk or the square, or in the web that we call the World Wide Web.

Typing something into Google is like boarding an aeroplane without knowing – although you think you know – what country you are heading for or which cities you will land in along the way. Just as we do when seated in the cabin, reading, watching movies, or simply thinking, once in front of the computer screen our fingers are filling our immobility with mobile journeys. Search histories and the trail of cookies draws a pattern of footprints – your own – through this personal and abstract city that we are all building by adding strata of likes, consumption, obsessions, secrets or conversations to the previous layers of our virtual biography. By surfing or browsing the net we are bringing our habits of wandering and roaming to the kingdom of the megapixel. These practices were invented by our long-lost ancestors and passed down to us in the way that we divide our time between countryside and city, keyboard and screen: our two lives.

Kurt J. Mac defines himself as a 'YouTuber roaming in search of the edge of *Minecraft*.' He could say that he is a miner who drills into the heart of the landscape of a video game, on the trail of a chimera: the 'Far Lands'. For the past three years he has been advancing in a straight line and sharing monologues about his thought processes with his followers. He does so because walking and thinking share a rhythm and because exploration (even exploration of the self) is meaningless without discourse. Kurt J. Mac is a *nom de plume*, of course. As a mask,

'I might be following people, all day long, every day, through all the streets in New York City. In actuality, following episodes ranged from two or three minutes when someone got into a car and I couldn't grab a taxi, I couldn't follow – to seven or eight hours – when a person went to a restaurant, a movie.' Vito Acconci about the *Following Piece*, 1973.

the name reminds me on the one hand of Joseph Conrad's Kurtz, at the heart of the Congo; on the other hand, it makes me think of a Mac laptop. It is a solitary business, but it turns those of us who are interested in his digression into Marlow, Kurtz's shadow, or at least into the shadows of Marlow's shadow. It is he who tells us the story of what happened during the event, in the pleasantly calm and immobile boat on the Thames, as he was reading *Heart of Darkness*. His adventure is neither voiceless nor absurd. It is not like that of the artist Simon Faithfull, walking in a straight line following the gridlines on his GPS in a pointless advance towards the boundaries of nothing. The stories, reflections, and jokes that constantly characterize Kurt J. Mac's walking have, by contrast, a meaning that he shares with his followers on a daily basis.

The couple Marina Abramović and Ulay decided to part by walking from opposing ends of the Great Wall of China until they met in the middle, and then said good-bye. 'We needed a certain form of ending, after this huge distance walking towards each other. It is very human. It is in a way more dramatic, more like a film ending.' Marina Abramović

Through them, his march becomes collective and political. Thanks to them – the people who have followed his five-part autobiography to date – he has raised over $250,000 for the charity Child's Play. Where is he walking to? Into the west. A pioneer can only make a pilgrimage to the Far West, although the ever-receding horizon is made up of pixels and algorithms and the programmers are constantly tasked with generating distance between the walker and a boundary that is becoming more and more impossible to reach.

Rebecca Solnit noted in *Wanderlust: A History of Walking* that 'journeys to raise money are already a North-American form of pilgrimage.' Kurt J. Mac's story is far from being the only one to have unfolded in the virtual sphere: in 2009 the workers at IBM Italy protested for employment rights in *Second Life*, while dozens of change.org protests have brought about profound changes in the real world. Solnit, who is an essayist and traveller, has given this summary of the turn of the new millennium: 'dialectics between the secret and the open; between consolidated and disparate power; between privatisation and public property; power and life, in which walking has always had a central role to play'. In *Wanderlust*, she displays enthusiasm for civil demonstrations, from London to Istanbul, Rio de Janeiro to Barcelona and Detroit to Tel Aviv, which have brought millions of people together to walk for a common cause. She notes that: 'the 21st century has marked the start of an era dominated by the power of people and public protests.'

Even solitary walkers like Rousseau, Thoreau, Benjamin, Norman, Chatwin, and Herzog have always had listeners, when night fell in their inns, albeit only inside their own minds, on the other side of the pages devoured by their readers. Don Quixote advances toward the sea with Sancho Panza. Borges wanders through the slums of Buenos Aires with Bioy Casares. Sami asks Ora whether he can accompany her in her disobedience, her radical refusal to say no, because we are all born ready to leave, ready to play the game and ready for company. Like so many other travellers, Sebald insinuates that he has no other reason for his journey than discovery; travel writing would not exist if we did not believe in the necessity of sharing our experiences of movement. In spite of the ubiquity of screens, or rather because of them, we are writing and reading more and more, and also walking and running with more dedication. This is how plots are woven – human, artistic, fun and political networks of physical or virtual game-changers – communities of walkers. David Grossman walked 500 kilometres to write his novel: it is a journey that thousands of readers continue to share.

fortably t

hrough pr

ages like

49   Inspired by a rebus 'ZA + patos = zapatos' translates into 'ZA + ducks = shoes,' this hand-painted
poster is the first of the poster series that Carlos Rolando created for the window display of the
Barcelona store (1981).

PONTELOS, MUÑECA. BOGART SE VA A VOLVER LOCO.

"Observa, pequeña. Zapatos de muñeca antigua. De tu pequeña muñeca. Ahora, sí, ahora mismo vas y buscas en el último cajón los calcetines de domingo de la academia de monjas. Y después, pequeña, márcate esos Camper. Y ven, que nos largamos ahora mismo a Casablanca, pequeña, (prefieres Ferry, DC-3 o Hispano Suiza?). Y nos desconectamos de la tele, del Mao, el Carter y el Fidel, todos juntos. Porque tú, muñeca, con tus pequeños zapatos de muñeca, vas a demostrar a todos esos tíos que passsas de todo. Por eso me vuelves loco.   Pequeña... Muñeca..."

CAMPER

SEGUN PASAN LOS AÑOS.

The advertising campaigns created between 1976 and 1979 by the design duo Lorente and Rolando were a blend of illustrations, photographs, a lot of text, sense of humour, and some good advice: 'Experiment. At Camper we use our heads to make shoes so that you can forget you have feet.'

51   'Hey doll, put them on. It's going to drive Bogart crazy' or 'Just imagine that Redford is massaging
your feet, Brando is working on your ankles, and Newman on your legs' are examples of slogans
used in ads from 1977.

Carlos Rolando
Graphic designer

'We established the four golden rules, when it comes to Camper's communication:
1. Never say the word "shoe".
2. Never use a photograph of a shoe.
Use your imagination.
3. Speak English. Camper is an international brand.
4. Use humour, make people smile.'

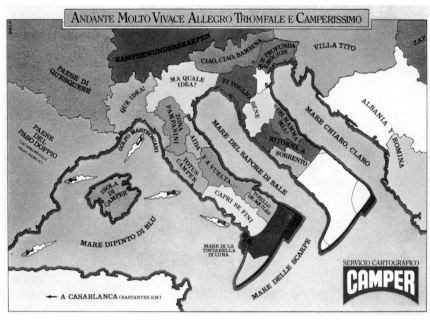

'The map of the two Italies' and 'The Palmera island' (1981) were among the first newspaper ads.

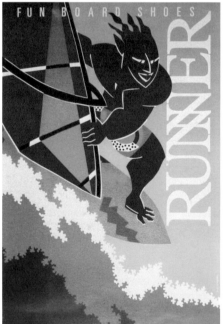

55   The posters for the store windows had a uniform format and were replaced monthly between
        1981 and 1993. Their subjects picked up on current trends, news, or traditions.

No insista. No los vendemos por separado.
N'insistez pas. Elles ne sont pas vendues
séparément. Don't insist. We don't sell
them separately. *Non insista. Non le*
vendiamo separate. *Bestehen Sie nicht*
darauf. Wir verkaufen sie nicht getrennt.

56   Twins are two different shoes that form a pair. Rolando summarised this concept in a poster he designed for the Twins' launch in 1992: 'Don't insist. We don't sell them separately.' The illustration is by his son, Mariano. The Japanese poster from 1984 was particularly successful, thanks to its message. A Japanese intern at Rolando's studio had added the slogan 'new Japanese art' to the sandal cut out from black paper.

57   Carlos Rolando was responsible for the company's graphic communication until 1992, when he was
      followed by Luis Bassat (Bassat Ogilvy & Mather). Oscar Mariné followed in 1996. The graphics
      of the Madrid-based designer were particularly bold and reminded viewers of superheroes: 'It's a bird,
      it's a plane...' (1998).

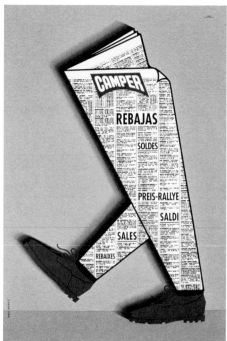

The posters in the bottom row are by Oscar Mariné. The ones on top are by Pati Núñez (1993/94).

59   'The other Spanish fashion', (Lorente/MMLB agency), was a take on the 'family and the state'
         campaign launched by the Spanish government in 1986 to promote Spanish fashion. The 'Pelotas
         by Camper. Keep them out of your grandparents' reach' poster and campaign date back to
         a design by David Ruiz and Marina Company from 1998, under the direction of Quico Vidal.

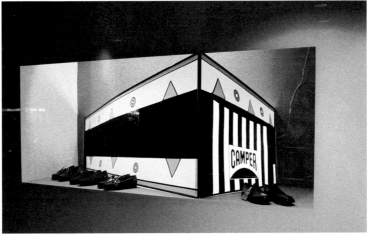

61   More than still lifes, shop windows are tools of communication. Examples of displays designed by Jordi Nogués between 1981 and 1995.

Some boxes were custom-designed for the model of shoes they contain, like the ones for Brutus (1984, top right) and Runner (1982), others feature feet of famous comic figures (1980, top left). For technical reasons Dutch designer Irma Boom's shoebox from 2007 (bottom right) never made it to the stores' shelves. Her design features a perforated exterior; the interior is printed with an image of Mallorca. In 1997 one box design was eventually selected for all shoes (bottom left).

63   The pink box with an atypical logo dates back to 1995. For the 20th anniversary of the brand Neville
        Brody created a new graphic system, which included a new logo, a new corporate typeface, and a new
        colour scheme. The design was launched and installed in the Floral Street store in London. But it did
        not last for long, as Camper returned to its well-established identity. Despite this episode, the Brody
        logo survived on the outsole of Camper's most popular shoe – the Pelotas Ariel.

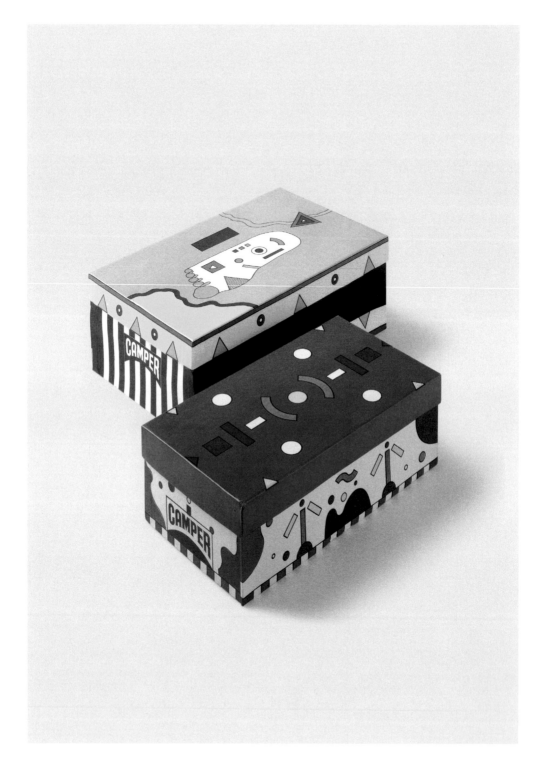

Among the most iconic boxes are the graphic bold designs by Nathalie Du Pasquier and George Sowden from the Memphis collective (1985). Du Pasquier explains: 'Our design resembled a poster but had the three-dimensional shape of a shoebox.' The two designers also created a unique postmodernist counter for the Barcelona store.

65   Designer and illustrator Javier Mariscal has regularly worked for Camper on graphic designs such
            as this playful idea for a bag for the Christmas holiday season. His work for the Camper for Kids
            collection (launched in 2006) is aimed directly at children, whom he considers more intuitive and much
            more creative than adults.

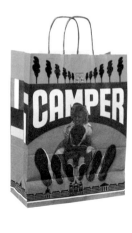

Camper soon understood that shopping bags are walking billboards. Usually they follow the seasonal designs of shoe collections – with some exceptions. The bag which features the Parisian skyline celebrated the opening of the first store in Paris in 1992 (top left).

67   In 1990 Luis Bassat introduced a new slogan: 'Me gusta caminar' ('I like walking'). This environmentally friendly statement was the next important step towards the brand's identity. It later evolved to become the famous 'Walk, don't run'.

Could we say that the act of walking is to the city what the act of speech is to language? Could we think of our feet as our mouths, articulating stories as we journey though the urban jungle? And in what ways are these stories writ and communicated? When we walk, we tread upon a dense palimpsest of those who have travelled these same sidewalks before us, each inscribing upon those pavements their own narratives. In this way, when we walk in the city, we are at once telling our own stories, while at the same time retelling stories of those who come before us.

Walking the city invokes a text, one that is instantaneously written while, at the same time, one that is instantaneously read. Michel de Certeau says, 'They walk – an elementary form of this experience of the city; they are walkers, *Wandersmänner*, whose bodies follow the thicks and thins of an urban "text" they write without being able to read it.' Walking is an act of reading the city with our feet. The city itself is an epic novel: each building a word, each street a sentence, each block a paragraph. De Certeau's claim for unreadability is hinged upon three facts: the blur of motion, the speed at which the tale is unwinding, and the sheer immensity of the text. When we speak of hypertexts, we usually mean those which exist online, but we might think of the city as the ur-hypertext, a dynamic analogue predigital model of complex intertextuality.

In the 21st century, the story has entered the third dimension. As we walk we emit streams of data, tracking where we're walking and how we're walking: how far, how fast, how many calories burned, and so forth. The air above the streets is thick with our narrative transmissions uploading to far-flung server farms where, parsed and analysed, they reappear on our devices in the form of maps and charts. This accumulation of data forms its own new urban palimpsest which is branded as the quantified self. But really, this data is not the quantification of the self, nor is it the quantification of experience, nor is it the quantification of narrative; it is the quantification of marketing.

We walk and we think; we read and we write. The rhythm of walking influences the pace of thinking. In a rush, we walk/think/read/write frantically and obsessively; at our leisure, we become literary flâneurs, pulled by the flows and currents of the urban environment, casting aside logic, letting our feet navigate the urban braille. When beset by his demons, Willem de Kooning would pace the dark streets for most of the night, walking as far south as Battery Park at the southern tip of the city and then back. Often he went on these prowls alone, but occasionally friends accompanied him. The critic Edwin Denby said: 'I can hear his light, tense voice saying as we walked at night, "I'm struggling with my picture, I'm beating my brains out, I'm stuck."' Relieving ourselves of intention, we get unstuck; drifting through the streets with a purposeful aimlessness, we find ourselves reading the city for pleasure.

Summmmmmmertime shoes.

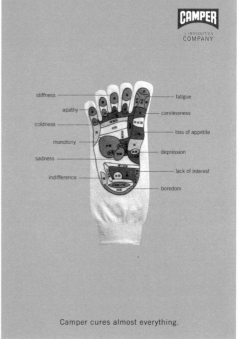

71   A carefully chosen image can convey an effective message. In 1999 and 2000 David Ruiz and Marina Company, under the direction of Quico Vidal, designed this series of posters with a simple, minimalist style. They featured the slogan 'The Imagination Company.'

Slogans condense the philosophy of a brand into a few short words and are messages that are easy to understand. 'If you don't need it, don't buy it' is one of the most unorthodox messages in advertising history (2002).

For the illustrations Martí Guixé used his unique handwriting, which he later developed into the exclusive typeface called 'Camper Casual' (2004).

75   The 'Walk, Don't Run' campaign presented an entire new chapter in Camper's communication,
       going far beyond product marketing. Camper became more than just about a pair of shoes
       or a lifestyle: the campaign took the brand at a slower pace and marked its more critical attitude
       towards the speed of contemporary (urban) life.

'The Walking Society' campaign was launched (2001). TWS implied a return to the rural origins of Camper and life in the Mediterranean countryside. The starting point was 'The Med is the net': a cultural network of people and places rooted in diverse social, cultural, economic, and geographic realities, yet united through their efforts to improve the world.

77   Under the direction of Shubhankar Ray and with graphic design by Pablo Martín, TWS took the form
       of a 'magalog,' a hybrid between a cultural magazine and a product catalogue. Six issues were released
       between 2001 and 2006, each one dedicated to a different location, starting with Mallorca and then
       travelling to Morocco, Greece, Italy, France, and Egypt. Together they painted a picture of Mediterranean
       culture. This community was reflected in the photographs of Stefan Ruiz and Jordi Bernadó.

WALK,
DON'T RUN

CAMINA
NO CORRAS

CAMPER®

BROTHERS
WWW.CAMPER.COM
T 00 44 (0) 207 409 31 30

THE
WALKING
SOCIETY

79   The success of the campaign led to explorations of regions beyond the Mediterranean, featuring markets such as India, Brazil, and China. A 'travelog' was created along the way to share images and sounds from these journeys via an online blog.

In 2007 campaigns focused once again on products and their special values, highlighting lightness, flexibility, comfort, durability, and quality. 'Imagination Walks' is based on the idea that every Camper shoebox contains a story and a pair of shoes to transport the wearer to a place called Imagination. It was devised by the Argentine agency Madre under the direction of Carlos Bayala, with photographs by Jean-Pierre Khazem.

81   A Peu ad on a bus in Paris. From 2008 to 2013 various agencies and authors were involved,
            including Julio Wallovits from La Doma ('Reinvent your Reality,' 2008); Swing Swing and Nadie
            ('Extraordinary Crafts,' 2010 – pictured, 'Lifelovers', 2011); and Toni Segarra from SCPF
            ('New Temples, New Pilgrims', 2013).

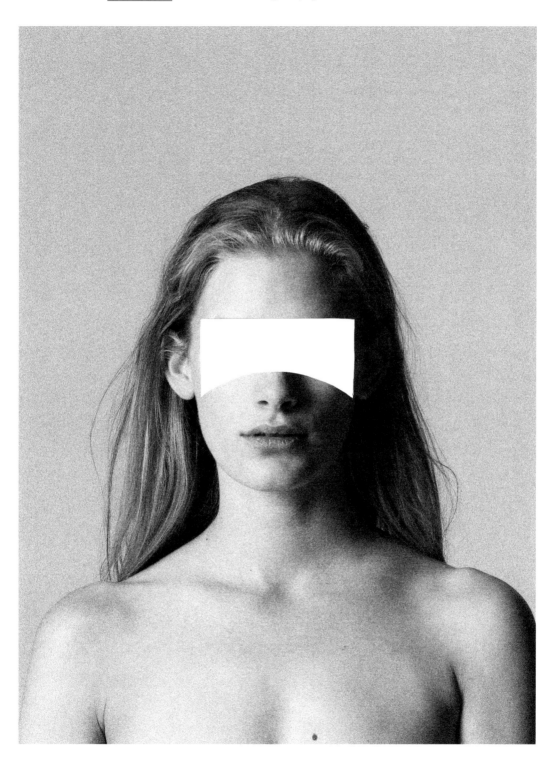

83   In 2012 Lorenzo Fluxa's son Miguel was appointed as the company's CEO. He is working to reinvent the brand to connect with customers who are closer to a younger generation. With this aim in mind, he called on fashion designer Romain Kremer as the brand's creative director. The stripped-down black-and-white campaign from 2014 reflects this change of direction.

In his book *Mythologies* (1954), Roland Barthes opened a new field of studies focusing on the social and cultural significance of mundane matters. Wrestlers' gimmicks, the shape of a haircut, the meaning of toys or a car became some of the founding myths that spread during the post-war era. Sixty years later, it is fully assumed that everyday life is built around a system of signs and artefacts that convey a great amount of information about contemporary social values. Some of them could even become long-lasting symbols, passing from one generation to the next. Adopting a Barthesian stance, how can we define the attributes of *camperism*?

In many ways, Camper visuals convoke an eclectic range of contemporary mythical figures. Since the post-Franco era, they diffuse assorted messages that participate in the creation of a new kind of 'peripatetic school'. The shoes are not only functional but they become the symbols of various ways of wandering in the meanders of our time. With regional nuances, witty tones, and the right dose of irony, *camperism* speaks out to urbanites sceptical about the progressive standardisation of cultural distinctions.

With models mostly concealed from sight, such communication seems intuitive in comparison to the marketing strategies that flourished during the 1980s and '90s. *Camperism* opens imaginary sidewalks where city-dwellers have an opportunity to weave between the obviousness and the pervasiveness of brand identities. Disparate, neutral, with an assumed lack of strategies, *camperism* has become a rallying umbrella for all kinds of drifters who ostensibly want to show their defiance to an increasingly branded world. The absence of an over-explicit corporate statement became a sign of integrity and,

[p. 80] The signification of the myth is constituted by a sort of constantly moving turnstile which presents alternately the meaning of the signifier and its form, a language-object and a metalanguage, a purely signifying and a purely imagining consciousness. – 'Myth Today'. [p. 88] The haircut, for example, half shorn, devoid of affectation and above all of definite shape, is without doubt trying to achieve a style completely outside the bounds of art and evaen of technique, a sort of zero degree of haircut. –

We are therefore dealing here with a humanized art, and it is possible that the Déesse marks a change in the mythology of cars. – 'The New Citroën'

by some means, its unsystematic approach allowed the company to adapt to the ever-changing world of tastes and signs.

Orthopaedic and anti-conformist, global and local, retro and hip, *camperism* is ubiquitous. Unlike many standard strategic planning practices, it can easily convey designations that can be morphed into diverse shapes and currents. This soft amalgam testifies that choices based on intuition are more than ever adequate in an era where styles and opinions are volatile. When more and more people are being forced to consider the fast track, *camperism* is an invitation to use alternative routes, the ones that currently run through the niches of deceleration.

'The Iconography of the Abbé Pierre'. [p. 333] There is a return to a certain degree of streamlining, new, however, since it is less bulky, less incisive, more relaxed than that which one found in the first period of this fashion. Speed here is expressed by less aggressive, less athletic signs, as if it were evolving from a primitive to a classical form. – 'The New Citroën'. [p. 83] Innumerable other meanings of the word 'myth' can be cited against this. But I have tried to define things, not words. – 'Myth Today'

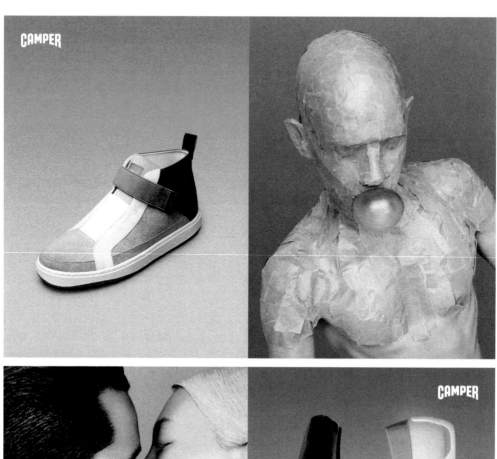

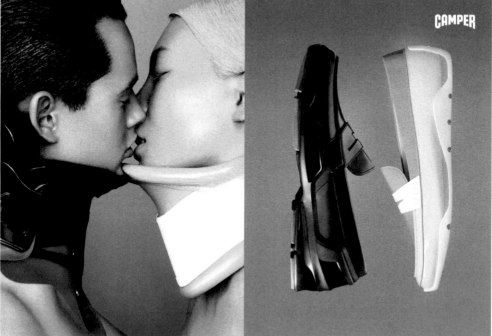

86   Images of the 2014/15 campaign shot by German fashion photographer Daniel Sannwald with graphic
design by A Practice for Everyday Life. The campaign in print and video plays with similarities between
shoes and their wearers, turning models, who were cast off the streets of London, into avatars, each
one representing a different shoe type.

An ad for the Mortimer shoe installed on Milan's Duomo (2015).

CAMPER

In the making of a campaign many aspects have to be taken into account: target groups, demographics, different cultures – and also superstitions. This white avatar was not used in advertisements for the Asian market because of her close resemblance to a ghost.

hese, slo

As a child, I vowed never to ruin my feet as my grandmother had: as a teenager in the 'Naughty Nineties', a decade that featured pointed toes and high-heeled boots and shoes, she had two bunions, several corns, and special soft glacé kid shoes to fit: plain black button-bar, low-medium heel, from the 1930s, when I first knew her, to her death in 1953. When I was old enough, she developed a 'bad' habit of waking me at 3.30 in the morning with 'Put your clothes on, we're going to London'. As a railway widow, she was entitled to cheap train tickets, so it was 4 o'clock milk train, breakfast at 6-something in Regent's Park, and then all the sights: the nearby Zoo, Westminster Abbey, Buckingham Palace, Trafalgar Square, and back home on the 7 pm train. My shoes then were black leather ankle-strap with a round toe, and a 1- or possibly 2-lift heel, which never seemed any bother, except twice on long Sunday morning walks with my parents when I complained that my toes hurt. My mother's answer was that they couldn't possibly hurt, as I hadn't had the shoes for long. But today when I dry my toes, I know I was right: just one toe on each foot did not recover.

After I began work in Northampton Museum in 1950, I searched for information to help interpret the shoe collection and everything connected with shoes. I discovered the long distances people had travelled, not just with the army or Crusades, but also clerics needing to go to Rome, who did not just walk there but went out of the way to famous places: to Italy via Vienna, making it the journey of a lifetime. There are many medieval pictures of the Virgin Mary with the Child on a donkey and Joseph walking alongside, usually in low ankle boots or high shoes, black, no heel, sometimes striding out with the forefoot appearing to strike the ground first (not the heel, which inevitably touches the ground first since soon after 1400 it was added to the sole, which was then a modest wedge or platform).

There are also the 'sandalia' worn by senior clerics in the Middle Ages, the Latin name deriving from the fact that they made the Roman sandal into an ankle boot, with four cut-outs from the top and a lace threaded through the top as drawstring, and very soberly foot-shaped. As with so many shoes up until the later 20th century, they were repaired, altered to fit different wearers, and then venerated. Shoes for most people were treated the same but were also changed according to new fashions in decoration, with a variety of pointed toe shapes to match the Gothic architecture we see in our old churches (some too long to be practical and liable to droop down in the stirrup when riding horseback). Uppers were one piece with the seam or fastening at the inside waist. Others were laced or buttoned in front, the button ingeniously knotted from a leather lace, leaving an end to be stitched on the inside. But when you look at the surviving bits, a different story emerges: single-soled turnshoes, the insocks usually missing or unrecognised, the sole often of two pieces, one of which is definitely a repair if the upper has expensive decoration, and both upper and sole often patched, at toe and sometimes at the back of the heel, which gives a clue to the origin of stacked leather heels ca. 1600.

An amusing and sad tale, which all shoemakers and cobblers (and their customers?) should read, is included by George Cruikshank in his 1842 *Omnibus*, entitled 'My Last Pair of Hessian

Boots'. I must first explain that these boots reached to the knee, the curvy top edged with gilt braid and the swinging tassel centre front, the back seamed, close-fitting at ankle and foot, elegant, expensive, and about to go out of fashion. The author obviously enjoyed flaunting them one day, only to find them replaced by a thief's worn-out shoes in the morning. He tried to find out what had happened to them: first a crack, then a lost tassel, then iron tips added and a new clumsy tassel; they had been to prison and to the pawnbroker, had been used by the driver of a hackney coach, and also used as a weapon; had been soled and re-soled, and then, having became one 'patch', were cut down to shoes (the legs kept to patch galoshes), and had then became slippers, until the soles were ripped off and sold to a poor man with many children who made a pair for them from what survived. Apart from George, all the rest made a few coppers, as did the cobbler and translator (then the lowest of the trade, who bought up old shoes, salvaged what he could and made 'new' shoes from the remains). Maybe this was not the fate of every pair of boots, but most were cut down and re-used. So when you see me struggling with an old shoe trying to work out what its original style and date was, you will understand when I say I really cannot be certain, but perhaps... [...]

Again until the late 20th century, the rich gave their discarded clothes and shoes to relations, servants or the poor, who might sell a fancy trim to make them more appropriate to their lifestyle. The much, much wider toes of the early Tudor shoes under Henry VII and Henry VIII again reflected the flattened arches in new buildings, and must have been a great joy to those who had suffered the medieval point. The leather, too, was more substantial for both upper and sole, requiring a method of sole-attaching, using a welt and sturdy insole, which our Technical College called the foundation of the shoe: a complicated procedure, so it took longer to learn the new skills, meaning opportunities for new people in the trade. Having become more delicate and refined during the long reign of Elizabeth, the white leathers did not survive burial, but fortunately were recorded in portraits. In her Warrants for 1595 the queen's Spanish leather shoes have 'high heels with arches', the first certain reference I have found for that extension under the sole we now call a heel (previously it had ambiguously meant the piece of upper leather round the heel of the foot). There had been platform soles as overshoes since medieval times, which from about 1405 were sometimes made a fraction higher at the back. When exaggerated in the 16th century into what Shakespeare called 'chopines', they were clumsy, and no longer practical to wear outdoors in English weather. So the removal of the spare bit between tread and heel, to make them lighter, also produced the covered 'Louis' heel, with at first, the sole continuous from the toe, up under the waist of the shoe, down the heel breast, and then under the heel to the back. About the same time the heel patches became the stacked leather heel: two types still familiar to us. And of course they inevitably changed the way of walking and added to our health problems. Now the heel hit the ground first, so shoemakers cut the sole to end at the bottom of the heel breast and added a separate top piece, easily repaired and replaced. They then discovered that heels sink into mud, a problem even in towns, but one that was solved by an overshoe: a mere 'toe-cap' with a flat sole attached, plus a 1-lift heel for easy repair. And then came an even more fundamental change: heels of different heights meant the shoemaker had to have lasts, not only of different lengths, but also shaped to the various heights, or the shoes were too uncomfortable. Considering the large additional costs, the only solution was to make the lasts and shoes straight, no longer shaped for right and left, a problem that lasted for two hundred years in England; this method, being cheaper, lingered on in parts of Europe until well into the 1920s.

The 17th century seemed to have more and longer wars than usual: the Thirty Years War on the Continent began in 1618. Wars require protection of the body as well as aggression, so boots were the major fashion: men must have felt impregnable with a strong boot to the knee and a softer thigh-piece to wear on horseback, or with boots turned down for off-duty swaggering, though the infantry and ordinary men in England's Civil War of the '40s had to make do with a high-cut shoe fastened through a single pair of lace-holes centre front. But plain practical, even with a red sole and heel (from 1610), did not suit for long, and it was then competing with the problem of how to tie the shoe at the front. Quarters (the back part of the upper) were extended into a short strap over the tongue (an extension of the upper). But then it was impossible to make them without a small hole at the sole end of the strap, soon exaggerated into an oval open side, with the upper only about 1 inch/2.54cm above the sole – not really practical, even when ignoring the latest fashion of tying them with a shoe rose (also

mentioned by Shakespeare); poorer folk made do with pieces
of ribbon. Open sides and roses continued under the reign
of Cromwell, who dressed as luxuriously as the Cavaliers.

Both these trends disappeared soon after Charles II was
restored to the throne in 1660, though there followed a brief fashion
for footwear with a big stiff bow tied at the front, a toe that was
square and tended to be shallow, and similar medium-high heels.
And then came the Glorious Revolution of 1688 when William
and Mary, joint rulers, brought in Dutch fashions: the square toe
curved into a 'dome', like the pediments over doors and windows
at that time, and solid heels of 4 cm or higher. We might assume
that ordinary people would be more practical, but in fact a man's-
size shoe survives with the 1660s toe and high heel, the sole worn
through to the foot, about ¼ inch/5 mm wide, right across the tread
between the stitching each side. Its last wearer must have had
no other choice but to go barefoot. And now, too, the women's style
started to diverge from the men's, adopting a more pointed toe,
which has been a curse for those of us with four long toes ever since;
I feel it marks the end of women's near-equality, conspicuous from
before 1066. Although the men followed suit in the 1720s, the toes
were rarely as sharp as women's, which curved up out of the way,
unused. [...] Men had also settled to the 1 inch/2.54 cm heel, worn
with only a few exceptions to the present day. More rounded toes,
and a few square, appeared with revolution in the air in the 1780s,
together with the return of rights and lefts – and a period of chaotic
styles, reflecting the unrest through to Waterloo in 1815, whose
anniversary we will celebrate soon. [...]

To state it quite simply, we need shoes. While we can usually make do without gloves, hats, or even bags, shoes serve the critical function of supporting and protecting our feet. Yet this is certainly not their only role in our wardrobes. Some women love the idea of wearing glamorous, towering stilettos every day, and many of today's most fashionable shoes seem more like sculptures for the feet than functional footwear. Luxury shoe designers are utterly unapologetic for being notorious for making sky-high heels that are difficult to wear. 'There is a heel that is too high to walk in, certainly,' Christian Louboutin confesses. 'But who cares? You don't have to walk in high heels.'[1]

We may not have to walk in heels, but we have to walk in *something*. While high heels are coveted for their femininity and sex appeal, the casual shoe – that is, the type of footwear that many women wear every day – receives comparatively little attention. We take for granted the multitude of shoe options that are in equal parts practical, comfortable, and stylish, yet women have not always had these choices. In fact, casual footwear as we know it today is relatively new to the sartorial story, having undergone important developments in Western women's fashion over the course of the 20th century.

In the early 1900s, many everyday shoes for women were, in fact, boots. They were typically made in basic brown or black leather, and rules of decorum dictated that they should cover the ankle and the lower calf, but other elements of their design varied. While it was acknowledged that boots with low, sturdy heels and wide toes were the most practical for walking, they were not always considered the

1 Christian Louboutin quoted in H. Freeman, 'Christian Louboutin: How Killer Heels Conquered Fashion', theguardian.com. (10 March 2010), http://www.theguardian.com/lifeandstyle/2010/mar/19/christian-louboutin-high-heels.

most attractive, and there were many options for alternative styles that featured pointed toes and curved, elegant heels.

Boots fell out of everyday fashion for women during the 1910s, and shoes stepped in as the predominant footwear type. This change was due in large part to rising hemlines, which, at an average of eight to ten inches (20–25 cm) from the ground,[2] became too short to reach the top of even the tallest boots. Now fully visible, the shoe became available in a greater range of styles. Colourful, embellished dress pumps were particularly appealing to consumers, but there was perhaps an even greater need for practical yet fashionable shoes. Such everyday shoe styles were essential for pairing with women's increasingly casual, modern wardrobes that complemented their more active lifestyles. A 1920 advertisement for the American shoe company George W. Baker declared, 'For informal dress, never smarter or more comfortable than today, one's shoes in particular must be easeful.'[3] The ad featured an illustration of a neat, front-laced shoe with decorative perforations; its modest heel was the only feature that clearly distinguished it from a man's brogue.

The feminization of traditionally masculine footwear was essential to many casual shoe styles for women during the early 20th century. In addition to brogues, which are characterized by their cap toes and pieced designs of perforated leather, oxfords (named for their association with the University of Oxford) were fashionable. The basic oxford style has a closed, front-lacing system and lacks perforated details, but it is otherwise subject to seemingly endless stylistic variations. Promoted as a walking shoe for its qualities of comfort and practicality, the woman's oxford was especially prevalent

2 J. Walford, *The Seductive Shoe: Four Centuries of Fashion Footwear*. Stewart, Tabori, and Chang: New York, 2007, p. 136.
3 Advertisement for George W. Baker Shoe Co., featured in *Vogue* (September 15, 1920), p. 132.

during the 1930s. The most versatile styles came in brown or black leather or suede, and had little or no ornamentation. There were myriad other examples, however, that featured colourful leathers and eye-catching details, such as cut-outs or colourful piping. Whether simple or more decorative, many women's oxfords had high yet sturdy heels.

'Loafers are functional shoes for your "come down off your high heel moments"' read an advertisement for Nettleton loafers in 1938.[4] A descendant of the soft-soled moccasin, loafers provided another casual shoe option for women. They were typically crafted from leather in tones of black and brown, and featured a hard sole with little or no heel. Nettleton's ad was printed two years after the American shoe company G. H. Bass introduced its 'Weejuns', a stylish take on a Norwegian farm shoe that was originally intended for 'loafing on the field'.[5] Although the first Weejuns were made for men, women quickly became interested in the style, and Bass debuted a feminine version two years later.[6]

The development of a variety of everyday shoes over the course of the 1920s and 1930s proved timely. In 1943, American *Vogue* featured an editorial on simple, low-heeled shoes that were crafted from a single piece of leather, noting that their construction was similar to that of a moccasin. 'In these days, with the nation on its feet, shoe-comfort is a matter to care about,' the magazine explained. 'We walk to work. We walk to win. We care about our shoes the way a solider cares about his guns. They must be soft and light, well-fitting, long-living... and handsome to be altogether right.'[7] Who better than *Vogue* to suggest practical styles that were also stylish?

4 Advertisement for Nettleton Loaders, featured in *Vogue* (November 1, 1938), p. 124.
5 G. H. Bass & Co, 'Our Story', http://www.ghbass.com/category/our+story.do.
6 N. MacDonell, 'Loafing Around: A Brief History of Fashion's Favorite Flat', *T Magazine* (November 23, 2012), http://tmagazine.blogs.nytimes.com/2012/11/23/loafing-around-a-brief-history-of-fashions-favorite-flat/?_r=0.

Variations on brogues, oxfords, and loafers continued to be fashionable throughout much of the 20th century – and they remain in fashion today – but the lexicon of everyday footwear was not yet complete. Another type of casual shoe took centre stage during the 1940s: the ballet slipper. This was not exactly a new idea, as there had been a similar fashion for soft, heel-less slippers during the first half of the 19th century. Modern ballet slippers, however, were generally much sturdier and more street-worthy than their predecessors.

A number of factors helped to popularize ballet slippers during the Second World War era. In the United States, they were one of the few shoe styles that was not rationed. They were also promoted by several prominent mid-century American fashion designers, most notably the sportswear designer Claire McCardell. Already known for her inventive, accessible clothing designs, McCardell approached Capezio during the early 1940s, taking some of her dress fabrics and asking the company to make ballet slippers to match. These shoes, as well as similar styles from other labels, quickly became fashionable for a multitude of occasions, and could even be worn with informal eveningwear.[8]

Women could also select from various other everyday shoes, including styles with low, sturdy wedges or platforms made in neutral-coloured leathers to match a variety of clothing. In 1949, the *New York Times* noted that the interest of fashion buyers at a trade show was 'especially keen in women's and misses' casual shoes'.[9] Clothing stores proudly advertised practical, relatively inexpensive footwear that could be located in shoe departments solely devoted to 'casuals'. In just a few years' time, however, the promotion of everyday shoes

7 'Fashion: The One-Piece Shoe', *Vogue* (February 15, 1943), p. 70.
8 'Feet on the Ground', *Vogue* (November 14, 1944), p. 110.
9 'Shoe Show Nears End with Buying Keen', *New York Times* (May 26, 1949), p. 46.

would be overshadowed by one of the most significant developments in the history of 20th-century footwear: the stiletto heel. When combined with a narrow toe (which it often was), the stiletto was an elegant, feminine, and unquestionably constricting style. Even if casual and comfortable shoes lacked sex appeal, they were in some ways more necessary than ever.

In addition to elegant loafers, the ballet slipper endured during the 1950s – and gained even greater status due to its association with the captivating French film star Brigitte Bardot. A trained ballerina, Bardot requested a pair of red leather ballet flats from the dance shoe company Repetto, which she wore in the 1956 film *And God Created Woman*. Bardot's girlish vivacity, combined with her raw sex appeal, provided a provocative new context for the simple ballet flat, one that foreshadowed the importance of youthful, easy-to-wear footwear styles during the 1960s.

By around 1965, dainty, feminine pumps were all but abandoned in favour of a 'new young fashion look'.[10] Fashionable 'baby doll' styles required shoes to match. This meant footwear with rounded or slightly squared toes and flat or low heels, which came in the form of Mary Janes, ghillies, strappy sandals, and – most importantly – boots. A design for flat-heeled, 'space age' boots in white leather, introduced by the French couturier André Courrèges, became one of the most copied styles of the decade. Sometimes referred to as 'go go' boots, this functional but highly fashionable design was ideal for the young woman on the move, and it paired well with the trend toward ever-shrinking skirt lengths. Yet 'go go' boots were not alone in their popularity. Flat- or low-heeled boots in nearly

10 'Rounded Toes Gain Fall Order Indicate', *Footwear News* (July 1, 1966), p. 15.

every style and height prevailed. Moccasins reemerged and were more directly influenced by Native American styles; in 1967, *Women's Wear Daily* reported on a collection by the young Yves Saint Laurent, in which the designer made the unlikely pairing of a grey and white tweed suit with fringed suede moccasins.[11]

The following year, Gucci launched its first line of women's loafers, reinterpreting a classic style for an eager new audience. The *International Herald Tribune* announced to its readers that they should consider flying to Rome just to purchase some,[12] and the company reported that 84,000 pairs of women's loafers had been sold in the United States by 1969.[13] Whereas Weejuns had always been affordable and especially favoured among college students, the new kind of loafers were considered status symbols, and were easily recognized by their metal hardware over the vamp. A perfected woman's shoe that is at once casual, easy to walk in, and luxurious – a trifecta of design – continues to be vital to today's footwear industry.

There was a pronounced shift toward 'unisex' shoe styles during the early 1970s, but making a feminine version of a masculine shoe was nothing new. Platforms were worn by both men and women, and while some soared to exaggerated heights, many had only small platform soles that were combined with chunky heels. These more modest styles provided some stability to their wearers, and were worn for a variety of occasions. Classic brogues and saddle shoes (a sporty oxford style that became a fashionable casual shoe during the first half of the 20th century) were modernized with vibrant, colour-blocked designs for both sexes. A 1972 editorial in *Footwear News* entitled 'The Guessing Game' arranged similarly styled

11 M. Russell, 'Paris Saint Laurent', *Women's Wear Daily* (July 28, 1967), p. 4.
12 S. Mower, *Gucci by Gucci: 85 Years of Gucci*. Vendome Press: New York, 2006, p. 19.
13 Ibid., p. 26.

casual shoes side-by-side, challenging readers to determine which were for men and which were for women. It was, indeed, hard to distinguish between the styles.[14] By mid-decade, fashion editors were announcing the demise of the platform in favour of simple designs with flat soles or low, stacked heels.

The design curator Louise Mitchell wrote that, since the late 1970s, 'the increased emphasis on casual wear has created a greater diversity of [shoe] styles'.[15] Similar to what had occurred during the 1920s, progressively less formal clothing was instinctively paired with complementary shoe designs – and the growing acceptance of sneakers as everyday footwear challenged existing casual styles. By the 1980s, certain shoe types that had formerly been considered casual – loafers being a prime example – suddenly seemed dressy in comparison to their rubber-soled counterparts, and they were worn in the office as well as for leisure. A more feminine everyday style was the basic, slip-on flat shoe, purchased by many women in practical shades such as black and navy. While these were two important examples of popular footwear, there were options (casual and otherwise) to suit any taste and budget. The plurality of shoe styles was especially striking in the following decade, when practical flats, combat boots and fashionable sneakers existed alongside dressier styles with platforms, tall wedges and stilettos.

In the late 1990s, the shoe designer Manolo Blahnik remarked, 'Flat shoes used to be associated with active or mannish women, like Greta Garbo. But today women have the freedom to wear mannish shoes. Women today have an incredible choice of different kinds of shoes.'[16] A number of high-profile shoe designers helped footwear

102   14 'The Guessing Game', *Footwear News* (May 11, 1972), pp. 6–7.
15 L. Mitchell, *Stepping Out: Three Centuries of Shoes.* Powerhouse Publishing: Sydney, 2008, p. 53.
16 Quoted in V. Steele, *Shoes: A Lexicon of Style.* Rizzoli: New York, 1999, p. 74.

to become the most important type of accessory in the 21st century, replacing designer 'it' bags. However, not just any shoe would do for many women. The first decade of the 21st century saw a trend for incredibly high, expensive, often elaborate heels. This vogue for 'impossible' shoes was especially pronounced in 2008, when the lowest heel in Christian Louboutin's collection was a staggering five and a half inches.[17] High heels are obviously fashionable, but how often are they really worn?

A recent study revealed that, although women have more shoes in their closets than ever before, 64 percent admit that they have purchased shoes that are too uncomfortable to wear regularly.[18] Not surprisingly, their pain-inducing selections include a great many pairs of high heels. Yet, as history has proven, we can have our stylish shoes and wear them too. Fortunately, some flat-soled styles have come to be considered as fashion-forward – or sometimes even more so – than their high-heeled competitors. 'Hallelujah! Shoes that are actually for walking and that don't rely on vertiginous heel heights for impact are gaining traction this season,' wrote the fashion journalist Elisa Anniss in late 2014. She went on to describe footwear with bright colours, metallic leathers, vibrant patterns, and contrasting panels that set them apart from familiar ballerina flats or brogues.[19] While it would be foolish to suggest that women will ever *fully* give up their high heels, it has long been evident that designers need not rely upon extreme heights to make fantastic shoes. As trends come and go, one thing is for certain: we will always need shoes that are made for walking.

103   17 H. Walker, *Cult Shoes: Classic and Contemporary Designs*. Merrell: London, 2012, p. 8.
       18 'You Probably Own Way Too Many Pairs of Shoes, Study Says', *Huffington Post* (August 19, 2013), http://www.huffingtonpost.com/2013/08/19/too-many-shoes_n_3779196.html.
       19 E. Anniss, 'Flat Shoes with Attitude', *How To Spend It* (November 3, 2014), http://howtospendit.ft.com/womens-fashion/67871-flat-shoes-with-attitude.

wly and v

105 Camper shoes are designed and developed in Inca, in the rural heart of Mallorca, by a young creative team of fifteen international designers. Far from the fashion centers, this team develops shoes that represent alternatives to conventional fashion trends.

106   Functional, even rational structures, shoes are closely related to the products of industrial design.
        But they also deal with questions of fashion, appearance, and the taste and personality that the wearer
        wants to communicate, a fact that cannot be ignored. Camper's designers have backgrounds in fashion,
        industrial design, handcrafts, and shoemaking. Their diverse approaches to shoes is reflected in the final
        collection.

107   The design process of shoes is a well-planned operation that runs on a tight schedule. Alongside twenty members of the technical staff composed of engineers, pattern and last makers, and craftsmen, the creative team develops two new seasonal collections eighteen months in advance.

'The creation of a shoe collection is an ongoing story. There are the plot basics, which develop from one season to the next. Then there are seasonal stories and styles. Inspiration can be found everywhere: from the excess of Mallorca's Magaluf to the idyllic beauty of Deià.'

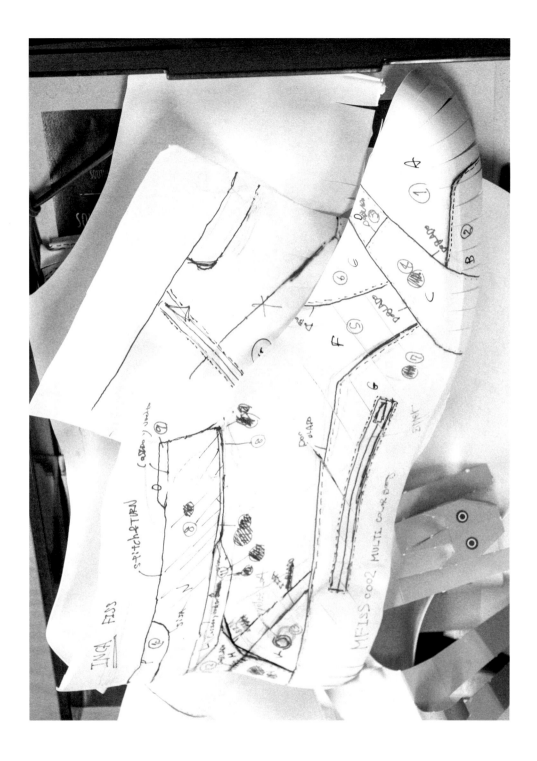

109   A three-dimensional sketch of the Fiss winter boot (2015) molded over a last – a mechanical form of a human foot. *Closca* (Catalan for 'shell') is the common name used to describe this plastic vacuum model.

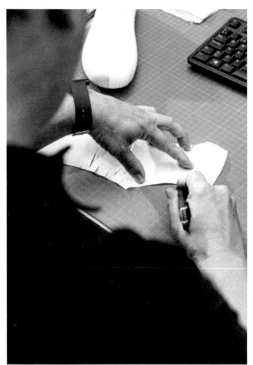

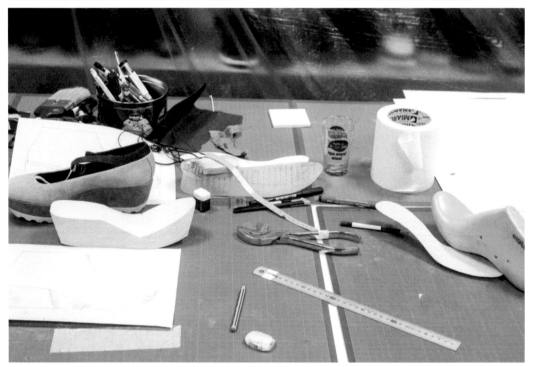

111   Plastiline, EVA, or, as in this case, masking tape are all tools of making mock-ups.

113   The starting point of each collection is a brief by the creative director and his team of trend, colour,
        and material experts. The brief is composed of colour references – about 20 to 25 – and material
        samples – over 350 – and, most important, of pictures and keywords that predict trends for
        the coming year's moods. These can be based on places (Alaska, Deià, Arenal, Es Trenc), materials
        (wood, ski, gemstones), even activities and objects (skis or inflatable swimming gear).

114   A designer approaches the design of a shoe as a holistic job, creating the object in all its elements, from
the upper to the outsole with its distinct graphic pattern up to the shoe's name.

115   Once the basic design of a shoe and its proportions are defined, the mock-ups are digitalized. Typically the last and outsole are 3D-printed and then combined with uppers made from softer materials. With new flexible plastic materials used in 3D technology, uppers can also be 3D-printed to create a prototype of an entire wearable shoe.
A foot model comes into the studio on a frequent basis to try and test these new prototypes.

116   In the past, black or brown leather suggested formal footwear. This classical order was altered by the spread of trainers, which made colourful synthetic shoes prevalent. Camper stayed faithful to its original idea of casualwear: the everyday shoe as an alternative to the sporty one without falling back to old-fashioned formalities.

117   Today colour and materials have broken free of pre-cast rules and even leather with neoprene or neon
           EVA or other unexpected combinations are presentable any time of the day.

Shoes, like chairs, are objects in which the idea of function is complicated by the competing claims of comfort and image. A shoe is not a garment, but it has an intimate connection with the body. It is not a piece of jewellery, but it can be understood as adornment.

The shoe is something that we wear for so many, sometimes mutually exclusive, reasons: to protect ourselves from the environment as well as to make ourselves alluring; for comfort, but also to demonstrate our social status. It is worn as an extension to the body, but it also manipulates the body. A shoe is mass-produced as well as handmade. It is the subject of constantly fluctuating social norms. For the first three quarters of the 20th century the British middle class were victims of arcane pieces of social lore such as the prohibition on brown shoes in the city. The state of the soles of a man's shoes was once seen as a reliable measure of his character, just as the colour of a woman's shoes, or the height of her heels, still is. The form of the shoe has evolved, as has the range of materials and techniques used in its manufacture. The casual has mutated into the formal. And of course, the shoe is usually worn as one of a pair: two objects that are closely related, but different.

The shoe can be understood as industrial design, as well as fashion. It can be examined from the perspective of anthropology and ethnography. The shoe is an object that is at the intersection of the body, and the world that it inhabits.

To design a pair of shoes successfully demands an understanding of the conventions on which they are based. But it also requires an openness to the speed of technical and formal innovation. In much the same way that utilitarian artefacts such as all-terrain vehicles or farm wear can migrate from their original purpose into fashion, so too can what were once highly specialized shoes, devised ostensibly for a specific purpose.

The industrialized way in which shoes are made has provided an equally enlightening insight into the nature of the modern economy, from the rationalist factory city built in the Bata dynasty in 1930s Czechoslovakia, to the outsourcing of the present day.

When I was a visiting professor at the Hochschule für Angewandte Kunst in Vienna, alongside Ron Arad, Helmut Lang, and Hans Hollein, each year there was a project set across the entire school. Every student was set the challenge by a skilled shoemaker of creating a pair of shoes. At the time, it seemed like an outdated reflection on the past.

But looking back, I see the exercise differently now. Understanding how to make a shoe, how to work with the materials needed to make it, and what the shoe does and means, is to explore every aspect of design.

120   This is the Zapatoteca. Camper's archive holds more than 6,000 shoes, prototypes, and experiments, which provide an important and ongoing source of inspiration for new designs. But it is not simply an archive; it's also the space where new collections are discussed, finalized, and laid out into different families.

121   Structured like a family tree, different shoe lines – also called concepts – are divided into styles and
        further branched into different options of materials, colours, and treatments.

123   Classic shoe typologies are called desert boot, oxford, derby, brogue, loafer, or slipper. A common
        approach of the shoe designer is to reinvent these typologies through amending – sometimes
        exaggerating – their volume, shape, and materials.

Often nonconformist, Camper has never aimed to please everyone. This attitude explains one of the reoccuring keywords of the latest collections: hybrid. Whether a shoe is composed of two different styles or a mix of materials, a hybrid questions the borders between formalwear and sports.

127   Camper has traditionally oriented its designs towards male customers. These models were later
        adapted to women's sizes. This brought about a focus on unisex shoes early on – a trend which is
        becoming more prevalent today, as the gender role in fashion and society is changing.

A private snapshot of a palm tree in front of Palma's cathedral was the inspiration for the jacquard fabric which became the print of a pair of Twins shoes for spring/summer 2014.

129   The Pelotas Capsule (2014) is a slip-on trainer style. As a spin-off of the classical Pelotas it has similar features to the original, such as the typical ball design on the thick cup sole, but with improved cushioning and grip. Its upper is a combination of leather and neoprene material.

131 Nonleather materials is an area of ongoing research for Camper. Looking for a water-proof alternative that has the typical lightness and pop-coloured puffy nylon look of retro ski jackets, the designers chose Gore-Tex as the material of the Fiss 2015 'winter sneaker'.

When we think of the 21st century, our minds often wonder through sterile environments, bright white surfaces, and transformative metallic structures – a dated image of the future inherited from mid-century technological advances and fantasies of space living. When we think of a foot, we think of bacteria, carbuncle and tenebrous, sweaty toe web spaces. It's fair to say, the foot was a fundamentally ill-fitting organism in 20th-century futurism, an antimodernist statement. However, the 21st century might yet be an era in which the foot, in all of its biological abundance, finally comes into its own.

Three vignettes offer a view on the evolving status of the foot in fashion – from 20th-century hidden appendage to millennial biomechanical apparatus, and finally to 21st-century bacterial microcosm.

In 1966, the foot was a hidden appendage

Cased in white PVC vinyl and block heels[1], the foot conceded to the minimal styling of the 'go-go getter girls!' and far-reaching goals of social progress as represented through Space Age fashion. It performed supporting acts of dance and march from the rather clammy interiors of a revolutionary boot 'made for walking'.

In 1996, the foot was a biomechanical apparatus

Framed for functionality between cushioning devices made of air, 'super' gases, energy return rubber and gels, the millennial foot was supported by a vision of the future based on techno-materials and engineering mastery. Running, jogging, breaking (swoosh)[2] – the foot was an athletic machine tasked with continual motion.

1 Pair of boots by André Courrèges, 1965. Search the Collections, V&A Museum, retrieved 17 March 2015.
2 Nike Air Max, Pair of trainers, 1992. Search the Collections, V&A Mueum, retrieved 17 March 2015.

So, what next for this human substructure that has so far been the hidden conduit of cultural ambitions and material progress? Here, we hazard a prediction for the 21st-century foot.

In 2026, the foot will be a celebrated bacterial microcosm

With the current microbiome revolution and the discovery that our bodies are 10 percent human and 90 percent bacteria and fungi, the foot's surface is celebrated as a garden of 'skin flora'.[3] Experimental designers are already responding to these ideas by making goo-set slippers that protect the vulnerable spaces between the toes, or by moulding shoe-forms using replicated layers of dry skin. This may well mark the beginning of an era in which the foot, as a lowly bacterial extremity, becomes a celebrated part of our microbial future.

 3 M. J. Blaser, 'The microbiome revolution', *Journal of Clinical Investigation* 124, no. 10 (2014): 4162-4165.

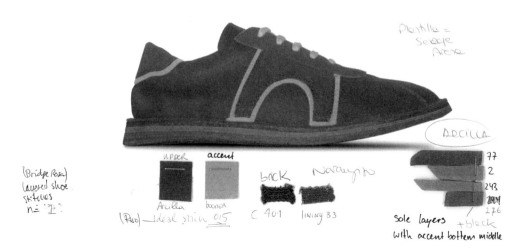

Initiated in 2008, Camper To&ether Shoes represent the individual approach of designers, as they reinterpret classic shoes or create new models. Some start from the production process or explore colours and patterns, others analyse the structure of the shoe. So did Hella Jongerius, who worked on several Camper shoes. She started with an almost scientific analysis of the various styles, revisiting colours and materials. The scope of her research was to find the 'imperfections' that give away the human hand in the industrial production process.

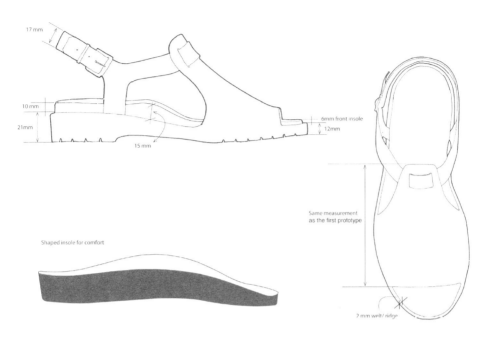

17 mm

10 mm

21mm

15 mm

6mm front insole
12mm

Shaped insole for comfort

Same measurement
as the first prototype

2 mm welt/ ridge

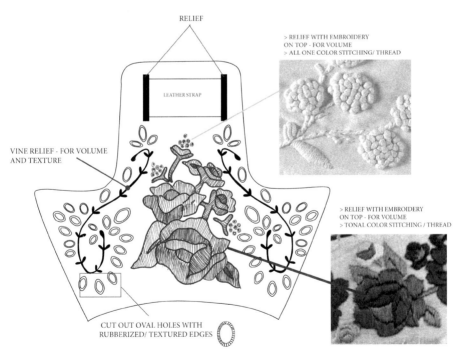

RELIEF

> RELIEF WITH EMBROIDERY
ON TOP - FOR VOLUME
> ALL ONE COLOR STITCHING/ THREAD

LEATHER STRAP

VINE RELIEF - FOR VOLUME
AND TEXTURE

> RELIEF WITH EMBROIDERY
ON TOP - FOR VOLUME
> TONAL COLOR STITCHING / THREAD

CUT OUT OVAL HOLES WITH
RUBBERIZED/ TEXTURED EDGES

135   Rachel Comey designs for women 'with a view to the world that is at once radical and romantic'.
             In 2014 she created a rubber summer sandal. The upper features a floral eyelet design which
             is hand-embroidered with raffia.

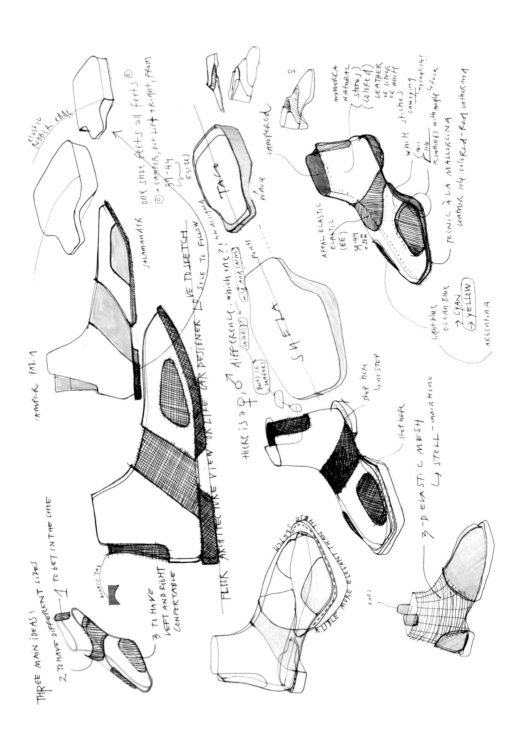

Swiss industrial designer Alfredo Häberli playfully reintroduced a galosh, a rubber slipcover that
protects the Campermeable (Spanish for 'raincoat', 2009) in the rain.
These sketches show how he manipulates shape to create a shoe that can be worn by both women and
men, and on either foot. The 'Unisize' concept, that adapts to fit sizes 39 to 44, was never produced.

Jasper Morrison's pencil sketches for The Country Trainer (2010). Conceived as a walking shoe, this model is simple and functional, true to the original Camaleón.

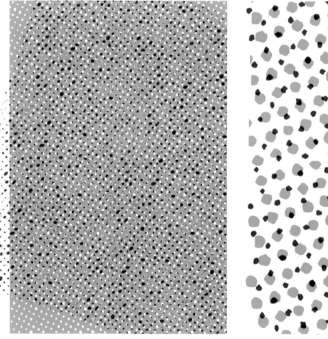

138   The fabric created by graphic designer Anthon Beeke for the Twins & Artists line is based on the
         idea of juxtaposing two primary colours at different print sizes, resulting in two versions of a basic
         dotted pattern at 2006 dpi and 1975 dpi.

C shoe

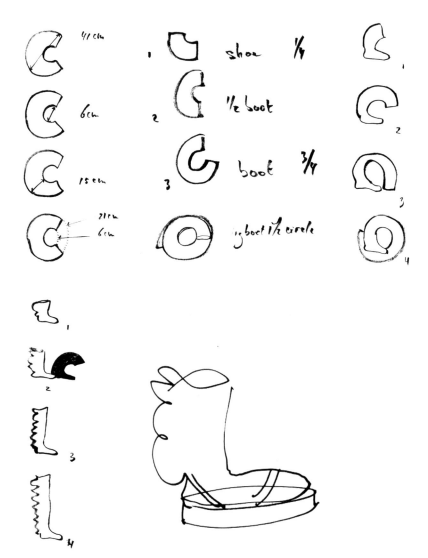

The idea of the C-shoe concept, drawn by Maria Blaisse, comes from the artist's work using recycled inner tubes (2008). Once transposed into leather, this doughnut shape became a highly original boot that fits like a sleeve with ruffles at the back.

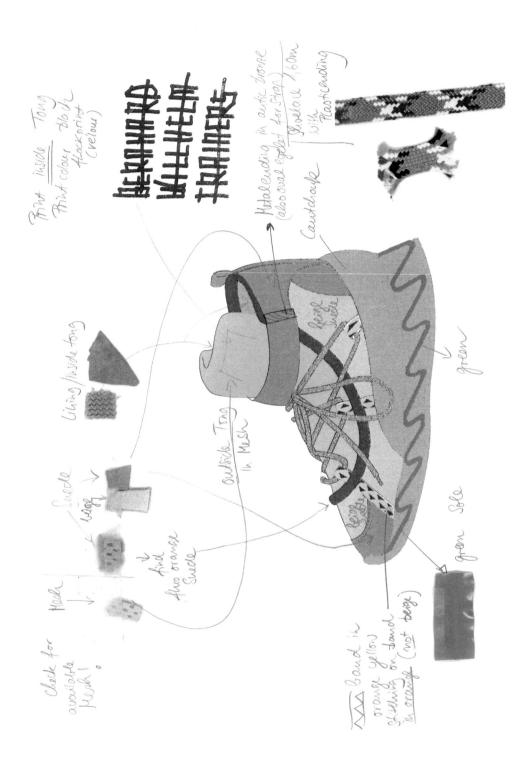

Print inside Tong
Print colour blah
Flockprint (velour)

BERNHARD WILLHELM TRAINERS

Metalending in artic bronze
(above oval eyelet for shop)
Shoelace 1,60m
with Plasticending

Cautchouk

green

green

Reine Suede

Beschichtet

Lining/inside tong

Suede

Wiss

Check for
available
Mesh!

Mesh

find
fluo orange
suede

outside Tong
in Mesh

Band in
orange yellow
stitching or band
in orange (not beige)

green Sole

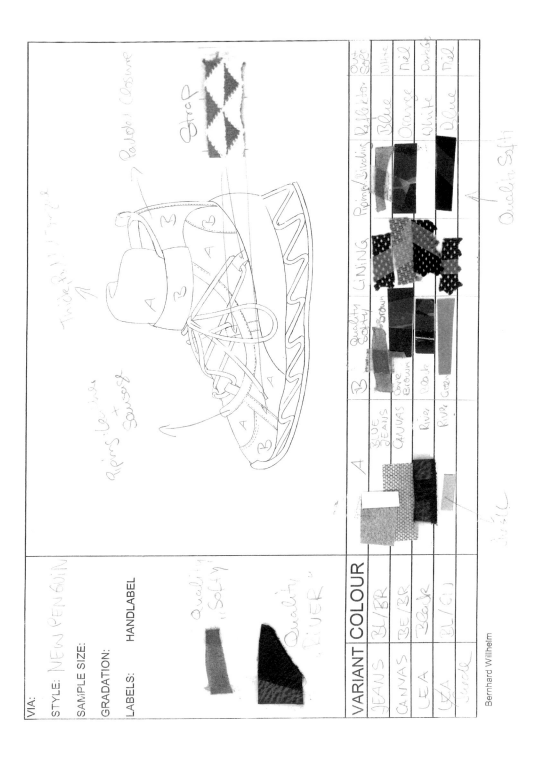

141   'Chaos is beautiful,' says Bernhard Willhelm. His design for the Himalayan (2009) is anything
but minimalistic. Some convincing was required before Camper brought the shoe out. It soon became
one of the brand's greatest icons.

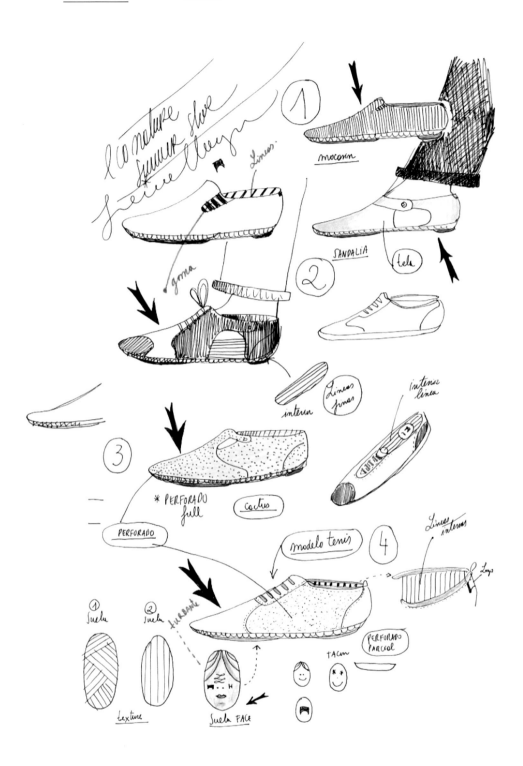

Imaginative sketches by Jaime Hayon for his first menswear shoes, which started the To&ether shoe
          collaborations.

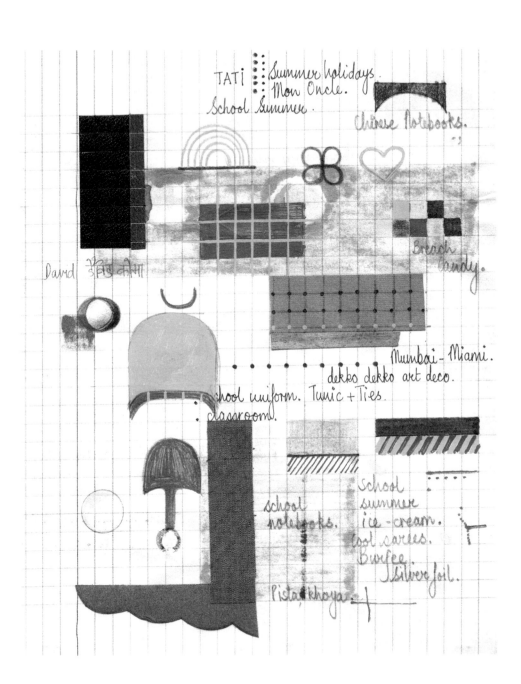

A page from a notebook of Nipa Doshi and Jonathan Levien for the design of a pair of Twins shoes (2013) with ideas ranging from art to Indian sweets covered with aluminium foil, school uniforms, and summer holidays.

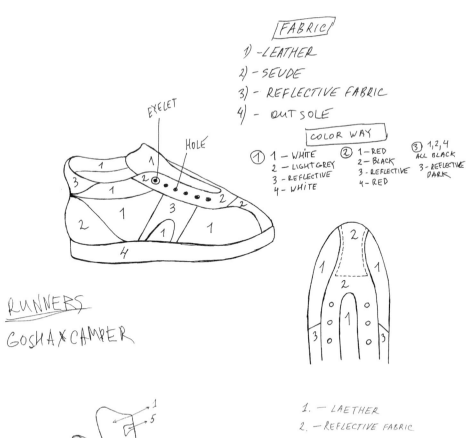

|FABRIC|
1) - LEATHER
2) - SEUDE
3) - REFLECTIVE FABRIC
4) - OUTSOLE

EYELET

HOLE

| COLOR WAY |

① 1 - WHITE
2 - LIGHT GREY
3 - REFLECTIVE
4 - WHITE

② 1 - RED
2 - BLACK
3 - REFLECTIVE
4 - RED

③ 1,2,4
ALL BLACK
3 - REFLECTIVE
DARK

RUNNERS

GOSHA✕CAMPER

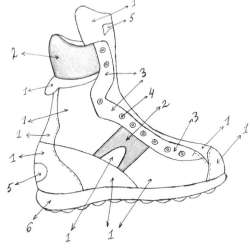

1. — LAETHER
2. — REFLECTIVE FABRIC
3. — SUEDE
4. — LACES HOLE EYELET
5. — LOGO RUBBER
6. — STANDART CAMPER

VARIANT A COLOR

1,3,4,5,6 → ALL WHITE
2 → GREY REFLECTIVE

VARIANT B COLOR

1,3,4,5,6 → ALL BLACK
2 → DARK GREY REFLECTIVE

GOSHA ✕ CAMPER SHOE AW/14
HI-TOP

Moscow-based fashion designer and filmmaker Gosha Rubchinskiy has declared that his clothes are designed for the generation born after 1991. His interpretation of the Pelotas and Runner (2014) were inspired by the youth culture, football, and skater scenes of urban post-Soviet Russia.

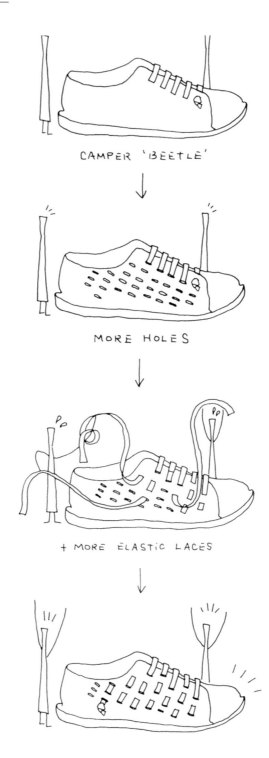

CAMPER 'BEETLE'

↓

MORE HOLES

↓

+ MORE ELASTIC LACES

↓

145   What's the essence of a Beetle? It's elastic lace that is secured with a knot on each end. In 2014
       Japanese design studio Nendo multiplied the idea of the elastic lacing weaving it into a cross-
       hatch pattern across the Beetle's upper. To date Camper has collaborated with more than twenty
       international fashion and product designers and artists.

146   There is a continuous search for perfect colours. In 2013 Dai Fujiwara, the former head designer
of fashion brand Issey Miyake, set out on a 'Colour-Hunting' expedition, travelling the world to create
a unique colour palette from nature, as an alternative to predetermined colour systems. The Lion shoe
(2014) was one result.

A colour experiment by Hella Jongerius (2009).

LAC15

CAC30

CAC08

CAC26

CAC24

149   Often the work of a shoe designer is similar to the work of a couturier, for example in the way he/she composes a card from different snippets and samples of materials and colours.

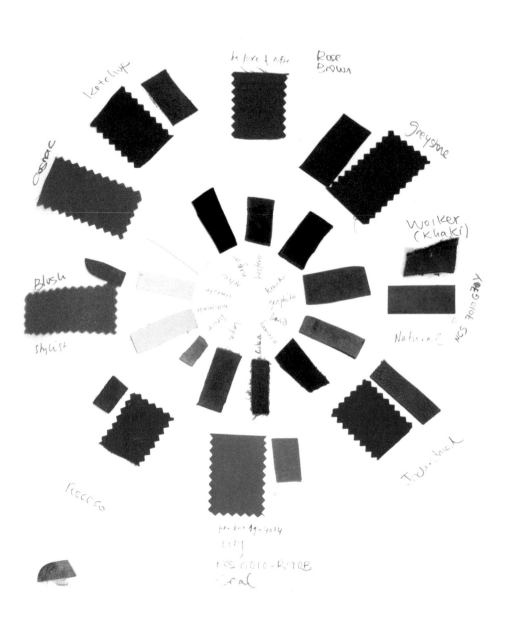

As one of today's leading colour experts, Hella Jongerius created a colour system and a colour wheel with combinations such as 'Balanced', 'Optimistic', and 'Misfit', which were applied to various seasons.

155   Lunch break at Camper's canteen.

Sporty, girly, slutty, androgynous… most shoes fall into very specific style types (or even clichés). But whether a shoe comes across as 'sporty' or 'slutty' is actually the result of a complex combination of factors: the type of construction, the shoe's features, colour, shape, and materials, as well as any cultural connotations the shoe might have, and where the shoe is positioned in the current fashion context.

In order to break these stereotypes – a must if we are going to be truly creative – we need to reimagine common shoe typologies, then open them up to a more diverse spectrum of contemporary shoe designs. Only in this way can we finally free women from the clichéd roles forced upon them.

One way to achieve this is by reinventing the process by which the shoe is made.

From 2011 to 2013 I held a Stanley Picker Fellowship at Kingston University. There, I approached the shoe from a purely scientific and technical point of view and set out to rethink the design method as a whole.

This method is based on research into the parameters required to support a foot (in a high-heeled position) while in motion. The defining or input parameters that the shoe needs to adhere to were taken from anatomic and kinematic studies of the foot and ankle. Based on these studies, I came up with seventeen hypotheses for high-heeled footwear possibilities that map out combinations of foot and ground contact points, which are necessary to (a) keep the foot in place; (b) keep the foot in its high-heeled position; (c) keep the object on the foot; and (d) the areas that touch the floor. Each of these parameters has an influence on the resulting design of a shoe, and will be the basis for a new logic in the configuration of shoe (elements).

In fashion, archetypes form the basis for design iterations. These archetypes are ceaselessly reinterpreted, recontextualized, and rereferenced. The object stays the same – or similar, but the way we perceive it changes.

One ubiquitous style, the brogue, perfectly illustrates this contextual shift. The brogue is a shoe that originated around 1580 in the farmlands of Scotland and Ireland and was constructed using perforated, untanned leather. This construction allowed water to drain out of the shoe when crossing wet terrain. The perforations, material, and look of the brogue have changed only slightly since their inception. But the original function and even its wearers (men) and place of use (the countryside) have changed completely. From the end of the 19th century, the brogue was considered a formal shoe appropriate for the office, and from the 1920s on, it became acceptable footwear for women. You would now be laughed at if found trudging through a wet field in a pair.

My question is whether it is possible to really generate new meaning when working with existing 'hardened' typologies. No, the codes that fashion is based on that have their roots in historic types cannot really change or become relevant through mere design iterations. To create new meaning, the object needs to deal with our current lives. In other words, we need to ask ourselves challenging questions like 'What is the relevance of trench coats in a time of drone wars?'

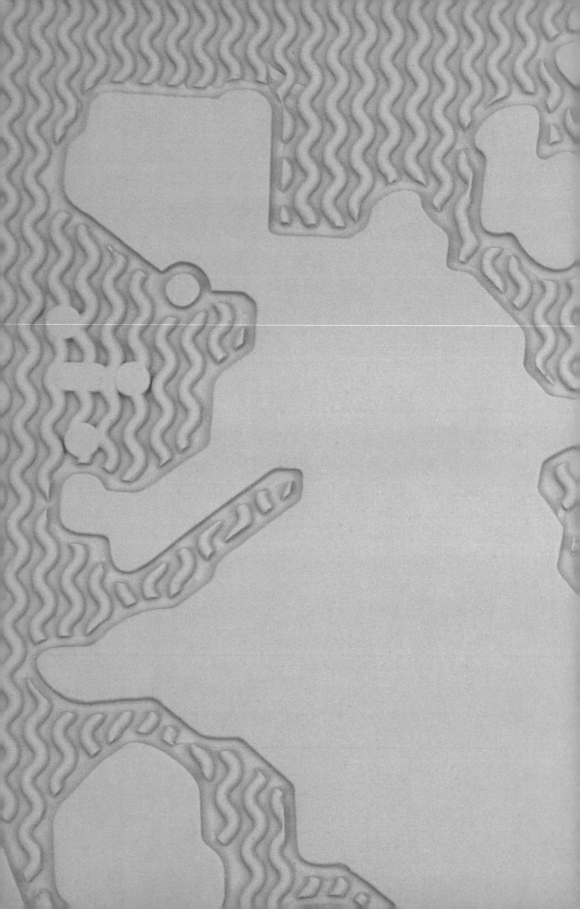

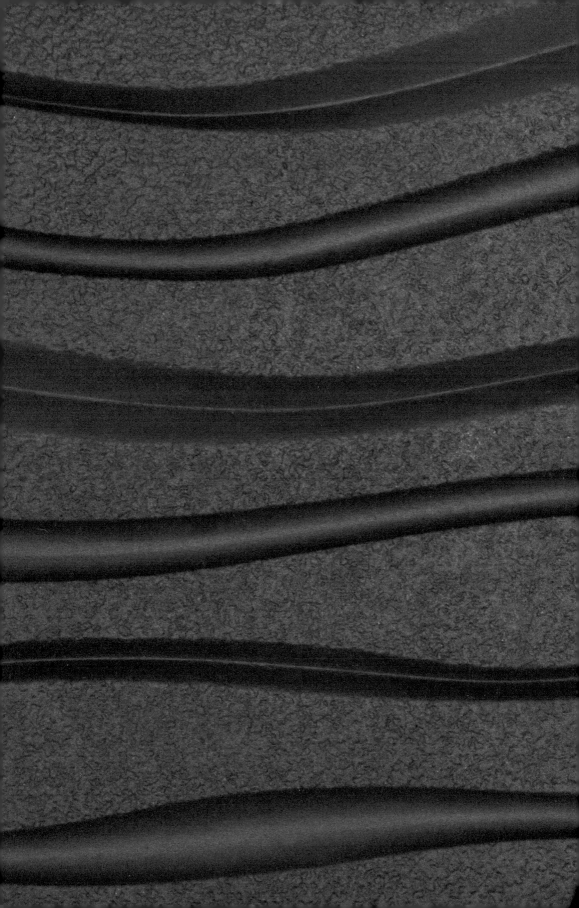